ACHIEVING PROFESSIONAL FULFILMENT

How to thrive in your career
and feel accomplished every day

Written by Virginie De Lutis
Translated by Carly Probert

Coaching 50MINUTES.com

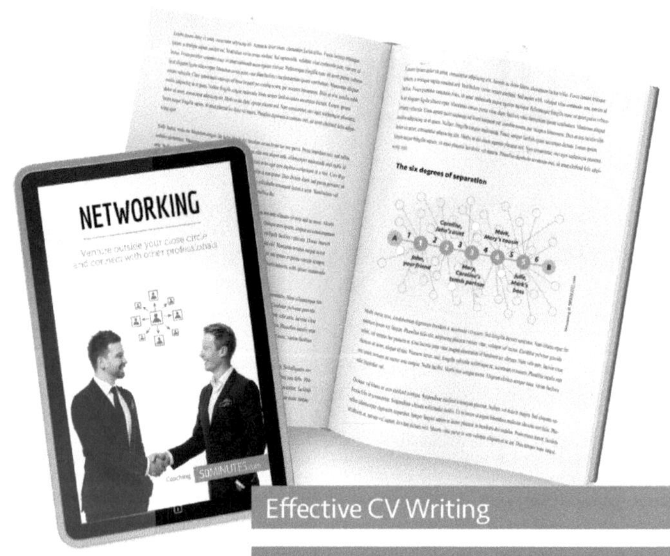

50MINUTES.com

PROPEL
YOUR BUSINESS FORWARD!

Effective CV Writing

Resolving Office Conflict

Boost Your Concentration

Find Your Work-Life Balance

www.50minutes.com

THE KEY TO PROFESSIONAL FULFILMENT

- **Problem:** How can I successfully create a fulfilling work environment, in order to arrive at the office feeling excited for the day ahead? How can I find a suitable, interesting and rewarding position in a professional setting?
- **Uses:** Work is where we spend most of our time. It therefore seems essential to be able to enjoy it and flourish.
- **Professional context:** Work psychology, work-life balance.
- **FAQs:**
  - What are the key elements that lead to professional fulfilment?
  - Is happiness at work possible for everyone?
  - How can I make a positive change?
  - How can I communicate with my boss?
  - How can I thrive in a toxic work environment?
  - What will my colleagues think of me if I quit now?
  - I'm worried that my colleagues think I'm a fool – what should I do?
  - Can I change jobs in the middle of my career?

While the unemployed continue to be demoralised, those who have jobs are told they should consider themselves very lucky. However, that statement appears quite relative if the job in question is not a source of fulfilment. Although work guides our lives and provides financial stability, it does not provide for all of our personal needs. It could even cause unhappiness that is difficult to put into perspective or eradicate.

Nonetheless, we live in a society where it is assumed that leisure time is a right. Some employers even use the harmony between private and professional life as an argument, offering the possibility of working from home or providing flexible working hours to suit their employees.

All that remains is to ensure the notion of professional fulfilment. What is this delicate balance that makes us look forward to the idea of going to work in the morning? How can we implement new habits based on one person, without negatively affecting an entire team? Is the value of one happy employee more than that of an unmotivated employee? How can we feel that we are in the right place and give meaning to our work? How can we make sure that we head home feeling accomplished, rather than crestfallen? In this guide we will look at how to do each of these things according to ten essential points, placing the key to professional fulfilment in your hands.

WHAT MAKES A FULFILLED EMPLOYEE?

In an ideal world, you would work on projects that are close to your heart, in a dynamic and friendly team. You would come home feeling relaxed, allowing you to enjoy your private life once you leave the office. Doesn't that thought paint a pretty picture? Unfortunately, this ideal world does not yet correspond with the one that we experience every day.

Stress related to job instability, lack of questioning or even a lack of imagination makes us forget that all that time spent at work is actually a time to which every human being must be able to give meaning. Of course, some claim to be satisfied with a big paycheque at the end of each month. Yet, it is clear that even the high earners are seeking mainly to achieve greater professional fulfilment that goes beyond their salaries. At the end of the day, money isn't everything.

Determining what makes us happy at work is a mission that can seem difficult when you have to juggle multiple parameters. You might feel uncomfortable, without knowing exactly what the problem is. This is likely to come down to a set of objectives that contradict and fight one another, and which are sometimes difficult to distinguish.

"Yes, but" – The game that slows everything down

If I asked you "Do you like your job?", you might answer with "Yes, but…". The psychological game of "Yes, but…" was popularised by Yves Lavandier in a feature film. It is actually a concept created by Eric Berne, the founder of transactional analysis. This game, played by two people, allows the person who begins his sentence in this manner to hide his emotions, drowning them in a cacophonous set of contradictory ideas. The "Yes, but" answer keeps you in a victim-like state, refusing solutions and stopping you in your quest for fulfilment.

Indications of a lack of motivation

Are you lucky enough to have a job? Are you happy to collaborate on a project that you find worthwhile or relevant? This is already a good start. However, you experience some of the following symptoms:

INDICATIONS OF A LACK OF MOTIVATION

- Stress upon waking.
- Weariness about the behaviour of some of your colleagues.
- Boredom at the idea of having to carry out your tasks.
- Annoyed looks at the clock, holiday calendar, Facebook, etc.
- Wanting to rush through tasks.
- Withdrawal, tendency to avoid exchanges with colleagues or superiors.
- Criticism of the company and colleagues.
- Boredom at meetings.
- Feeling of being demeaned or under-estimated.
- Feeling that your abilities are not used to their potential.
- Returning home in a state of exhaustion or irritation.
- Impossibility of taking your mind off work.
- Etc.

Professional Fulfilment © 50MINUTES.com

The list of indications of a lack of motivation goes on and on. Being surrounded by colleagues who are at the same stage as you is terrible for morale. Therefore, beware, because the risk in this situation is that your condition will deteriorate further and put you in an awful state. Successfully identifying the origin of your discomfort is the first step towards change.

NOTE FOR EMPLOYERS

There are some behaviours that make it possible to notice a lack of motivation in an employee: higher expenses, taking office equipment home (lack of respect for business assets), arriving later or leaving earlier. These indicators may reveal the need to return meaning to their work. The ability to listen then becomes the greatest tool for re-creating a nurturing environment with this employee.

Factors of professional fulfilment

Several factors of fulfilment are observed in happy employees. Among these are:

Motivation factors
• Giving meaning to what you do • Feeling useful • Having the possibility of being creative • Holding decision-making power • Personal progression • Making fewer errors • Knowing the projects you are collaborating on • Being recognised by your colleagues and superiors

Using this list or a list of your own, determine what objectives would motivate you in your workplace. Then you can easily decide where to focus your efforts.

Set your goals

To be able to feel fulfilled in the workplace, many employees are willing to accept lower wages. The key here is to determine whether money is an objective in itself, i.e. if the main focus of your working life is not to contribute to your life, but to maintain a healthy bank balance.

Other objectives are indeed possible. Perhaps you are the kind of person who is fascinated by analysis? Does your taste for discovery and ingenuity prompt you to challenge yourself? You are likely to need a job that puts you in contact with new topics that require deep thought. In this case,

Professional Fulfilment © 50MINUTES.com

repetitive work is not for you. Choose a career that matches your aspirations. If you find that your schedule is a problem, your goal may be to find a job with flexible hours, which respect and value your family life. It is important to list the things that are problematic now so that you can turn your attention to the conditions necessary for the fulfilment of your goals.

PSYCHOLOGISTS' VIEW

An article in the *Journal des psychologues* explores the results of a study on French teachers. The author, Pascale Desrumaux, discusses the concept of welfare at work and writes: "In the workplace, employers have a duty to ensure the welfare of their employees".

Business is all about profitability. To achieve this, it relies on the quality of productivity. This is only possible if the employees work in a state of wellbeing, so it is logical for employers to make this one of their primary concerns. Wellbeing and discontent are essential components to the success or failure of a business. Finally, companies are responsible for their employees, and therefore their physical and psychological states.

VALUES AND BELIEFS

Values

Values reflect our principles, our vision of what is right and wrong in society. They are expressed by our actions and our way of being. To feel good, it is necessary to develop in a system that shares our values, including, but not limited to:

- respecting commitments with regards to customers;
- quality customer service;
- a certain tolerance for the mistakes of colleagues;
- the need to improve and to learn;
- etc.

Beliefs

While values are concerned with right and wrong, beliefs affect what you perceive as true or false. They result from your life path (family, immediate environment, experiences), but also from our society. They unconsciously guide our choices and decisions. Within a company, a belief system is established. Adaptation is natural if there is no dissonance between these beliefs and our own.

If you feel tense or experience any discomfort about performing certain tasks, it is possible that you are trying to juggle two opposing belief systems. For example, you may think that "unity is strength", while your company pushes you to see your colleagues as competitors. Or you may even see your salary as an earned merit and are prepared to do many extra hours to earn more, while your boss wants premiums to be equal for all employees.

This opposition of beliefs can push you to:

- deny a problem and then find that it keeps coming back;
- change your own behaviour and cause a stir in the company sphere;
- fall into cynicism ("That's typical") or self-justification ("I have no choice").

It is therefore essential that you ensure your actions agree with your thoughts. By going against your beliefs, you are causing frustration or annoyance that will eventually make you insane (contempt, lack of self-esteem, etc.) or affect your attitude (disloyalty to the company, non-flow of information, etc.).

EXTRA INFORMATION: LIMITING BELIEFS

It may be that your discomfort affects a limiting belief: this is what you think you have permission or the ability to do, obtain or be. This is the little voice that tells you that you cannot succeed, that you do not deserve to grow or that you will never be as good as your colleague. Listen to it carefully, and then try to turn it into a motivating belief.

THE IMPORTANCE OF BEING YOURSELF AT WORK

To thrive, we need to be ourselves. Do not try to be or appear like someone else at work. Of course, this is not the same as being who you are as a parent, child, or friend.

Try to visualise your "professional self": What are your skills? What are your needs? Would you like to undergo training? Do you want more responsibilities? Do not try to excessively please others or endorse a role. Develop a healthy personality, armed with professional skills. If you are shy, do not try to force yourself into anything, but try to move towards other people. Likewise, if you are more of an extrovert, don't hold back.

Express what you hold in your heart, what you think of things and projects: give your view on solving a problem. But beware, there are moments when it is better to take a step back. For example, do not speak out in anger or over-reveal your private life.

Some people, mostly women, complain of having an appearance that does not inspire respect. To compensate, they force themselves to dress up in outfits that they consider "serious" and build a professional profile that takes them away from their core personality. If you find yourself doing this, inquire about psychology rather than the exterior of personalities. Increase your confidence and treat this problem before displaying an appearance that ultimately corresponds to a false image of yourself.

Being yourself at the office will help you to feel more free and achieve a certain level of wellbeing; two essential things in your professional development.

ANOTHER FAMILY

Sometimes companies become like a second family. The quality of our relationships with our colleagues plays an important role in our professional development; a good atmosphere is always more enjoyable and productive than a tense atmosphere. However, pay attention to your psychological position and ensure that it is making you happy. Be careful not to exploit your work relationships, reproduce a pattern, or compensate for imbalances you show or have shown in your private life.

BE SELF-CONFIDENT

Fulfilment without self-confidence is an impossible dream. This confidence is necessary to act and undertake new challenges, but is also important in your relationships with others. Therefore:

- **Try to take better care of yourself.** Feeling good about your body will help with your mental wellbeing. If you want to play sports but cannot find the time, tell yourself that ten minutes a day is better than nothing. If you think that you send a bad image, make an appointment with an image consultant. With regards to your diet, have you thought about changing it? Each person must find the dietary lifestyle that suits them. Following this logic, the internet is full of practical advice and coaching advice.
- **Accept your mistakes and do not beat yourself up.** Learn from those mistakes and you will move forwards. Once you have made an apology, you need to turn the page and ignore the criticism or ridicule from your colleagues.
- **Have an open and frank attitude.** Force yourself to express yourself when you are faced with events that do not suit you. If you are shy, do so without arguing at length. Humbly show what you think.
- **Accept compliments.** They are all good to take. Since we all have qualities and defects, why deprive yourself of recognition? If you feel that you don't deserve them, keep this state of mind to yourself and be content with giving a "thank you". You will have time to analyse what your colleagues value.
- **Positively claim your place in your company.** Be proud of your work and be aware of the fact that by claiming it, you are happy with the role you play within the company. It is not pretentious to describe reality: your place in the company counts and you enjoy holding your position.

NOTE FOR EMPLOYERS: "THE RULES OF INTELLIGENT SIMPLICITY"

According to Yves Morieux, the associate director of a large consulting firm, the current management systems are obsolete and damage workers, causing disengagement, burnout and bad relationships. He thus establishes "six rules of intelligent simplicity" that aim to improve the work environment and performance:

- Understand what your colleagues do in the office;
- Enable business managers to enhance employee actions;
- Increased the decision-making power of employees;
- Take account of the near future and the impact of service quality or the company's products;
- Encourage cooperation between colleagues;
- Do not blame people for their errors, but because they did not ask for or offer help.

BE AWARE OF YOUR ADVANTAGES

Your assets in the professional world comprise your knowledge, skills and useful traits in your work. Therefore, being aware of them will allow you to enhance your strengths as an employer:

- Question their added value by comparing your profile to potential opportunities in the job market. For example, your skills in a certain type of software may be obsolete, but does your profession still interest you? Do not let these gaps stand in your ways and stay up to date with the many courses on offer. Don't hesitate to improve your skills and advance in your profession.

- Ask yourself if these strengths make you happy. For example, are you good at accounting, but dream of working in a garden? In this case, stop thinking about what you can do and learn to do what you think is right for you.

We often ignore or devalue our own assets. If you are of a discrete nature, for example, highlight your delicacy, your listening skills or your analytical fineness. Retaining a staff member often allows a team to work more harmoniously. If, in another case, you feel like you are the one who moves forward, think about your capital gain for the company: is it not because of you that each issue is discussed in depth? Do you now have the ability to go further than others when it comes to thinking about all the parameters of a problem?

THE MBTI

The MBTI test (Myers-Briggs Type Indicator) is a patented global standard that identifies 16 psychological profiles (the test is free to do online). It gives you guidance on your way of relaxing, thinking, understanding events and making decisions. The profile it reveals is extremely interesting, and it helps you to get to know yourself and be able to confirm your way of thinking or retrain it accordingly.

WARNING

If you see a promotion available, consider the Peter Principle, which states that in a hierarchy, every employee tends to rise to his or her level of incompetence. Your talent can make you climb the ladder and gain access to functions that do not correspond to your skills or desires, so keep an eye on changes in your position. On the other hand, why not take advantage of your expertise by training your colleagues?

The Peter Principle

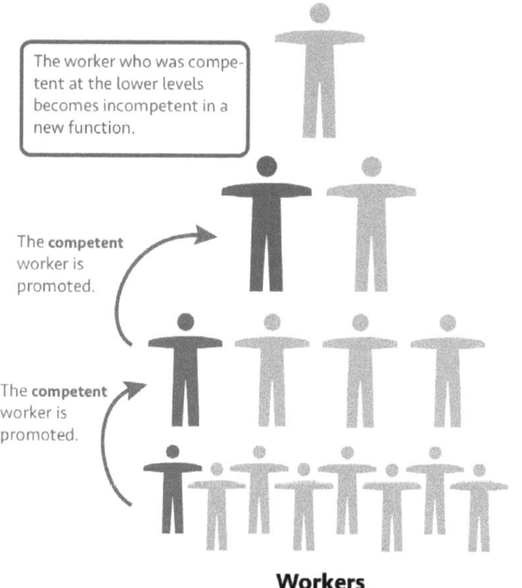

COMMIT YOURSELF FULLY AND REMAIN OPTIMISTIC

> "Choose a job you love, and you will never have to work a day in your life." – *Confucius*

Passion can be an essential element in professional fulfilment, as it makes you forget about the stress of your job. An exciting job is a job that matches your personality and your strengths. In short, it is a job that suits you.

However, is it necessary to be passionate to be happy? No. Rest assured; although passion plays a role in our personal fulfilment, it is not essential to our happiness and we can thrive without it. If you do not feel any particular passion for your job or the position you hold, commit yourself 100% to everything you do and, above all, have fun. If you are bored, try to find new challenges that will stimulate you.

Another important element is positivity. In a video broadcast, psychologist Shawn Achor argues that happiness does not come from success, but from positivity. The feeling of happiness creates additional resources, making us more efficient.

Give the best you have, believe in yourself. Develop everything that has value in your eyes. Numerous scientific studies have shown that a positive person is more efficient and more profitable than a negative person or somebody with a neutral temperament, so smile with confidence today.

In his book *Trop de coachs crèvent de faim* (*Too Many Coaches Die of Hunger*), Alain Samson concretely describes the actions needed to advance his coaching career, but states that these tips are also applicable to anyone developing their own business. Whatever stage you may be at, you are asked to imagine yourself as the boss of your own business. Your one and only product is you, what you are and what you are capable of. This is what you sell every day to the company that employs you. It is a beautiful product that deserves success. If you have trouble considering selling yourself at a good price, read this sentence from Alain Samson which will perhaps change your opinion: "Selling is the ability to transfer enthusiasm" (p. 36).

BALANCING YOUR PROFESSIONAL AND PERSONAL LIFE

We all know that this balance is essential to our growth, but we all find ourselves, from time to time, using the famous "Yes, but..." that contradicts common sense. You want to preserve your privacy, but:

- the meeting next week is crucial;
- your boss is watching you out of the corner of his eye;
- your colleagues give you a chance to shine through their disengagement;
- you believe in your work;

- you must give 100% to reach the next level that you
  envisioned.

All these reasons may be relevant or not. What makes the
difference is the impact on your wellbeing. Indeed, if you
favour the professional sphere at the expense of your personal life, perhaps someone is suffering from your absence
or distance? Do your children see you enough? Does your
husband feel supported? Does your wife often feel alone?
While it is good to set professional goals, they must consider
your environment. According to the jargon of coaches, this
is called "eco-logic". Be ecological: set limits and align them
with those that feel the consequences of your professional
dedication, so as not to regret them later. Here are some
tips to help you achieve this balance:

- Know how to say "no" when you are overworked.
- Take several breaks during the day and take a real lunch
  to recharge.
- Take part in activities outside of work (play sports, go to
  the movies, etc.).
- Take stock of your personal or family life: are the people
  around you happy with the time you spend with them?
- Do not reveal your entire personal life when at work,
  keep confidences for your friends.
- In return, try to see your colleagues for who they are and
  appreciate the positive features of their attitudes.
- Avoid gossip and remain professional in all situations.
  Work remains work, and should not be transformed into
  theatre.
- Your work is not necessarily your passion: develop activi-

ties that interest you outside of the office.
- If your health is endangered by your work, take control and address this immediately.

IMPORTANCE OF HEALTH AND SAFETY

Health is an essential part of your life. This may seem obvious, yet:

- have you thought to check that your chair is suitable and allows for good posture?
- is your screen comfortable on your eyes?
- is there enough light in your office?
- do you remember to drink water and eat a real meal at lunchtime, instead of a quick snack?

Make your own observations and take time to think about your health and note any risks. Basic recommendations (posture, screen, breaks) are essential in the long run because your body will remember if you have abused it. Check-ups with a doctor will give you an objective view of your current state.

Safety is governed by standards and the legal framework for all activities must be respected. Whether physical or legal, safety in your workplace must be guaranteed. Do not take the standards that have been set by professionals lightly, as they have often been set in response to past situations. By paying attention to them, the dangers that your employer might put you or your colleagues in will be minimised. Do not hesitate to consult your union or other organisation serving workers if you feel concerned about any aspect of safety.

TOP TIPS

- Get regular updates on your situation and take a step back. Are you happy? Are you smiling? If not, what is lacking or making you uncomfortable? Learn to identify what does not suit you, then make an updated list of goals that will help you to apply yourself.
- Take the time to read or think about your goals each morning. Think about what is making you tense. In every detail of your day, search for an opportunity to embody this fulfilled person that you want to be, both physically and mentally.
- Be consistent and realistic. You cannot ask for more responsibility, and more free time: you cannot have everything. If you want to avoid becoming frustrated, you must sacrifice some of your desires and make concessions.
- Be creative and take the lead: give your company the best you have. Prepare, argue and defend new projects. Share your desire to progress.
- Take care to distribute the tasks you are most excited about throughout your schedule so as to find positive feelings regularly. Manage your time to nurture positive thoughts and change your habits if necessary.
- Create authentic moments of conviviality with positive colleagues. If you are trapped with toxic or slanderous colleagues, try to focus on what this is doing to you. Many resources exist to analyse human relationships, inform you of what attracts you and if you have a problem, analyse the unconscious games you play. Understand what attitudes are having a negative effect and identify

how to get out of these games.

- Be efficient: burnout is not a state, but a process. If you spend your time complaining about your job, or have no other focus, start to question your surroundings. Are you stuck in a rut? Have you lost your joy of life? If necessary, consult a coach or therapist.
- Set yourself limits. If, despite your efforts, your work is weighing you down, there are only two options: take it or leave it. Determine a deadline to analyse if the job can help you to thrive; apply yourself fully to your actions in order to improve the situation. When the big day arrives, decide and take ownership of your choice. If it is only the position, and not the company, that does not suit you, try to talk to the human resources manager to find a win-win solution.
- Treat yourself to time and space. Take time to rejuvenate and improve yourself. Only after rest – a real rest – can you project yourself in the future to meet your aspirations.

FAQS

WHAT ARE THE KEY ELEMENTS THAT LEAD TO PROFESSIONAL FULFILMENT?

By questioning yourself and your motivations, as well as what seems most important in your work, you are already halfway there. All that remains is to focus on every detail to make the most of them. During this reflection, do not eliminate anything that might seem ridiculous or illegitimate. It is only by honestly establishing these two lists that you can identify what motivates you and what would help you to thrive.

IS HAPPINESS AT WORK POSSIBLE FOR EVERYONE?

It certainly is, although it comes at a price. No situation is without drawbacks. The key is to choose those that cost you the least. For example, if your health no longer allows you to keep up with the pace of work imposed by your current job, resign, even if it may seem tedious. Being transparent and taking responsibility for your choices is key.

HOW CAN I MAKE A POSITIVE CHANGE?

There is no better time than now to take action; things can always get worse, but this is not within your control. However, it is up to you to take control and make improvements. Enjoy the positive details of your day, and don't miss out on a thing.

HOW CAN I COMMUNICATE WITH MY BOSS?

Do you want to change your schedule or your responsibilities? Your boss should already be listening to you. If you state your point with conviction, dedication and enthusiasm, your boss will listen to your proposals with interest. If the change does not suit them, you need to evaluate if this is really what you want for your professional life.

MY BOSS IS RELATED TO ME

Emotional ties that develop at work can become difficult to untangle. If choosing between loyalty to a parent/relative with whom you work costs you your health or joy of living, question yourself on the value of that emotional connection.

HOW CAN I THRIVE IN A TOXIC WORK ENVIRONMENT?

Unfortunately, this is not possible. If you have sincerely tried to bring positivity to your business environment and ultimately have made a firm decision that the problem lies with the system, give up. If your financial or family situation does not allow you to resign, deploy the necessary means to achieve your new goal: finding another job.

WHAT WILL MY COLLEAGUES THINK OF ME IF I QUIT NOW?

Do not group all of your professional experiences in the same category. Each departure is the result of a process in which you are not the only determinant. In addition, the person you are today has more experience and maturity. This person now needs to flourish, and that's all that matters.

I'M WORRIED THAT MY COLLEAGUES THINK I'M A FOOL – WHAT SHOULD I DO?

Be the fool. If you have decided instead not to be the office clown, to have more responsibility or stop gossiping during your coffee break, act accordingly. Abandon the role you were assigned to by the team. Visualise the person you want to be and stick to this image. The feeling of being in the wrong scenario will gradually fade away.

WARNING!

Any change will cause resistance, firstly from yourself. Then comes the resistance of others, which could provoke the same from you. Do not view them as obstacles, but as steps that you need to take in order to reach your goal. Do not let the unrest of those who liked you better "before" slow you down. You have decided to apply yourself at work with determination and concentration, so go for it!

CAN I CHANGE JOBS IN THE MIDDLE OF MY CAREER?

Think of all those who have done this out of conviction or obligation: everything is a question of motivation. It may be that you are looking for a way to end a painful situation, or simply that you have realised that your job does not interest you anymore. If you are attracted to a different kind of job, many courses are available in the evenings or online to redesign your career.

OVER TO YOU

This visualisation exercise will not take long. Imagine that a year has passed. Yes, one year after reading this! You have made the necessary changes and are even happy at work. How would you respond to these questions?

- What three things make you happiest in your work? (Earning more money, serving a useful cause, coming home from work early, being highly regarded by your employees, your potential, etc.).
- What has changed in your private life? List three elements. (You go home happy, you have more time for your loved ones, you are less tired, you have a new hobby, you dress differently, etc.).
- How do you feel about the idea of having succeeded in changing your professional life? (Do you trust yourself? Are you relieved? Do you not understand why you waited so long?).
- What damage was caused? Why? (Your family has less income? A colleague wanted you to be put forward?).

Re-read your answers and focus your attention on your physical sensations. Do you feel breathless? Are you relieved? Does your face light up?

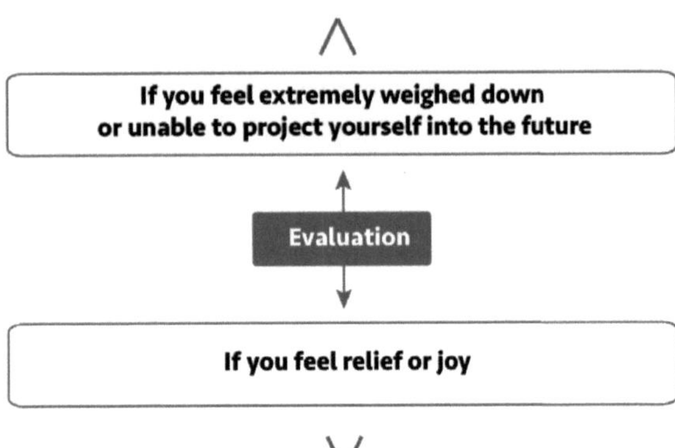

Professional Fulfilment © 50MINUTES.com

PROGRAMMING YOUR FULFILMENT

Do not ask about the exact date when you will change: you have already set out on the road to your goal fulfilment by reading this book. Enjoy your momentum as you move forward step by step.

Name one concrete action to implement over the next three days which will allow you to get closer to this new target.

This may be a small thing (taking a break outside, reorganising your desk, etc.) or a large step (making an appointment with a doctor or coach, preparing a new draft to be submitted to your boss, buy a book on a related subject, etc.).

TOMORROW MORNING: COMMITMENT

When you wake up, believe in yourself. Put a sticky note on the bathroom mirror if necessary and tell yourself that you are the happiest in the office. If this is not yet the case, it will be soon.

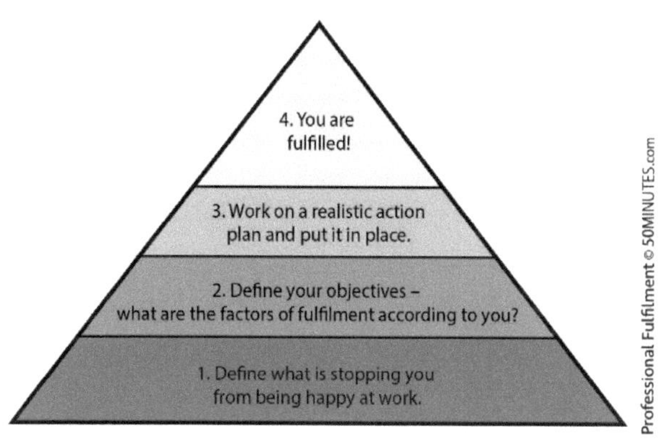

We want to hear from you!
Leave a comment on your online library
and share your favourite books on social media!

FURTHER READING

BIBLIOGRAPHY

- Achor, S. (2011) Shawn Achor: The Happy Secret to Better Work. *Ted.* [Online]. [Accessed 25 July 2015]. Available from: <http://www.ted.com/talks/shawn_achor_the_happy_secret_to_better_work>
- Ariely, D. (2012) What Makes Us Feel Good About Our Work? *Ted.* [Online]. [Accessed 25 July 2015]. Available from: <http://www.ted.com/talks/dan_ariely_what_makes_us_feel_good_about_our_work>
- Desrumaux, P. (2010) Le travail, risque psychosocial ou facteur d'épanouissement? *Le journal des psychologues 10/2010. Cairn.* [Online]. Issue. 283, pp. 26-30. [Accessed 25 July 2015]. Available from: <http://www.cairn.info/revue-le-journal-des-psychologues2010-10-page-26.htm>
- Pepin, C. (2013) *Platon La gaffe, Survivre au travail avec les philosophes.* Illustrations by Jul. Brussels: Éditions Dargaud.
- Morieux, Y. (2013) As work gets more complex, 6 rules to simplify. *Ted* [Online]. [Accessed 25 July 2015]. Available from: <http://www.ted.com/talks/yves_morieux_as_work_gets_more_complex_6_rules_to_simplify>
- Samson, A. (2011) *Trop de coachs crèvent de faim.* Canada: Beliveau Éditeur.
- Verbroomen, G. (2014) *Le seuil d'incompétence de Peter.* Namur: Lemaitre Publishing.
-

ADDITIONAL SOURCES

- Arte TV website:
  http://info.arte.tv/fr/le-bonheur-au-travail>
- Monsempes, J-L. Le Bonheur pour réussir. *Institut Repère.*
  [Online]. [Accessed 17 August 2016]. Available from:
  <http://www.institut-repere.com/Videos/le-bonheur-
  pour-reusir.html>
- MBTI test website:
  http://www.analyse-transactionnelle.com/Mbti/Mbti.
  html>
- Winget, L. (2013) *Arrête de te plaindre et bouge-toi.* Paris:
  Leduc.s éditions.

FILMS AND DOCUMENTARIES

- *The Secret Life of Walter Mitty.* (2013) [Film]. Ben
  Stiller. Dir. United States: Twentieth Century Fox Film
  Corporation.
- *Le Bonheur au travail.* (2015) [Documentary]. Martin
  Messonnier. Dir. France: ARTE France. France.
- *Oui, mais...* (2001) [Film]. Yves Lavandier. Dir. France:
  Canal+.
- *Stupeur et tremblements.* (2003) [Film]. Alain Corneau.
  Dir. France: Canal+.

50MINUTES.com

History

Business

Coaching

IMPROVE YOUR GENERAL KNOWLEDGE

IN A BLINK OF AN EYE !

www.50minutes.com

© 50MINUTES.com, 2016. All rights reserved.

www.50minutes.com

Ebook EAN: 9782806279286

Paperback EAN: 9782806284358

Legal Deposit: D/2016/12603/381

Cover: © Primento

Digital conception by Primento, the digital partner of publishers.